How to Quickly Get Started As a Personal Coach

Get Paid Big Money To Change People's Lives

Christian Mickelsen

Christian Mickelsen

Christian@CoachesWithClients.com

619-320-8185

San Diego, CA

Limits of Liability and Disclaimer of Warranty

Warning – Disclaimer

ISBN-13: 978-1490997148

ISBN-10: 1490997148

Contents

Coaching Quiz: Want to know if you'd make a great coach, go to http://www.CanICoach.com and take the 60 second quiz.

CHAPTER 1
What Is Coaching?

Q: What is coaching?

A: The facilitation of growth and change.

There are a lot of different definitions for coaching. You can scour the Internet and go to different coaching schools, coach training programs, and coaching associations, and they all have different definitions of coaching. If you ask 10 different people in the industry "what is coaching?" you'll probably get 10 different answers. Some people define coaching in a very narrow way. There's this profession called therapy and this other profession called consulting, and coaching is the fine line in between. But, I don't look at it that way. I have a very broad, yet simple and powerful definition of coaching. I think it's just a fantastic definition—by far the best I've heard. Of course, I'm probably biased. Many people are very uptight about the definition of coaching. They hold it sacred and put coaching into a tight box. I destroy the box!

The way I define coaching is the **facilitation of growth and change**, and anyone or anything that facilitates growth and change is a coach. There's a saying: everything and everyone around me is my teacher. I believe the same is true of coaching—everything and everyone around me is my coach. Everything and everyone around me facilitates my growth and change. Especially books, movies, friends, family, and even the guy who cuts me off in traffic. And of course, my own personal coach.

Now I get coached by my wife and by my daughters. I get coached by the conference call recording company that didn't record my calls properly. I have to learn and grow from that either by learning patience, understanding, or forgiveness. Anyone or anything that facilitates growth and change is a coach.

How does coaching differ from consulting? Coaching is about teaching somebody to fish, as opposed to consulting which is doing the fishing for them. In coaching, you identify what people want, what their challenges are, and you show them you understand what they're going through and how hiring you would help them overcome the challenges and get what they want. Coaching is more about the client and what they want and need rather than about you and what you bring to the table. Your skills are definitely important, but it's more about how you can help them.

How does coaching differ from therapy? The big difference to me between coaching and therapy is that coaching is about helping people get what they want, and therapy is about helping people overcome what may have happened to them in the past. People who have experience in the counseling field should not practice therapy, because you could get in trouble for doing therapy without a license. You can coach, though, without any licensing.

Q: What is a professional or personal coach?

A: Anyone who gets paid to facilitate growth and change.

While coaching is the facilitation of growth and change, there is a difference between what is coaching and what is professional coaching. Professional coaching (also called Personal Coaching) involves anyone who gets paid to facilitate growth and change. While we may randomly grow and change from experiences in life and from people we meet in life—such as someone we meet who changes our lives forever—there are people who get paid specifically to help others grow and change.

Some specific types of growth and change that people often hire coaches for are:

- business growth

- getting into a relationship

- turning around a relationship

- starting a business

- finding the right career

- finding meaning in life

- making sound executive decisions

- getting employees to work well together

- facilitating a smooth merger

Q: How does coaching work?

A: Generally the coach helps clients achieve goals.

There is no exact formula for what happens in coaching. And depending on your training and experience, your coaching process will vary. In general, when a professional coach has a "coaching session" with a client, a few things happen. First, the coach finds out how the client wants to grow or change, which usually involves goals like starting a business, getting a better job, finding a mate, making more money, losing weight, etc. Sometimes the clients will know exactly what they want, and sometimes figuring it out is part of the coaching process.

Next, the coach and the client create a plan for achieving these goals. They may also identify the challenges that could stand in the way of successfully achieving change, and they figure out a way to address these challenges.

Then, they will measure progress. Is the client moving closer to the desired result or not? If yes, it might be worthwhile to investigate how the process could be sped up. If the client isn't getting closer to the desired result, the coach and the client discuss where the breakdown could be. Is there a problem with the plan, or is the plan not being followed properly, or is the client afraid of something and feeling "stuck"?

The process of checking in and helping the client stay accountable and on course for change will go on until the client feels like progress is steady and there are no "bumps in the road" or until the desired result is accomplished. But, most clients are often working on more than one goal at a time. So, even when one area is going well, there is usually a lot more to work on.

This is a big simplification of the coaching process. There's a lot more to it, but it doesn't take a brain surgeon or a rocket scientist to figure it out.

Q: What is the format of coaching?

A: It varies, but most coaching is done through weekly phone sessions.

There are a lot of formats for coaching. Remember that coaching is the facilitation of growth and change. With this in mind, coaching shows up in various shapes and forms. The premium version of coaching is one-on-one coaching either over the phone (or video chat using a service like Skype) or in person. Many coaches do one-on-one coaching and also work with clients in small groups. Usually, group coaching will revolve around one goal that all the participants have in common. However, what is commonly thought of as "coaching" is one-on-one over the phone.

Some coaches meet with their clients in person. There are certain things that I like to get together with clients to do occasionally, but the phone works really well. The more I got into coaching, the less I drove to see anyone. I've never had a client say, "I'm not going to hire you unless I can meet with you in person." There may be people who think, "I could hire Christian out in San Diego or Jane who's right there in my area who I can see in person." I may have lost some business, although it's not very likely.

Actually, I had someone tell me they met a coach locally they were going to hire, but even though they had never met me, they felt more comfortable with me and felt a better connection with me so they decided to work with me by phone instead of the local coach.

There are a lot of advantages to phone coaching. It's more convenient for the coach and the client. The coach can work with clients all over the world. You can move your business any time or even coach from the beach! There's no travel time for you or for the client, and you can get right on the call, get right off the call, and get right on to the next call—maybe even take a little break or whatever. The client can get right off the phone with you and get right into action on whatever you were coaching on. They don't have to drive home and get distracted and then try to get refocused and maybe lose that momentum. That's a big benefit. It saves them time and energy because they didn't have to drive anywhere.

Also, another benefit is a level of safety people feel. Have you noticed that by e-mail people can say the craziest stuff that they would never say to your face? Over the phone is somewhere between e-mail and in person. In person, they may feel a little bit more judged, a little bit more intimidated. Over the phone, there are things we can do as a coach to make them feel a little safer. In general, the phone feels much safer than in person. I always conduct the initial interview with new clients over the phone so there are no visual filtering or biases affecting you—you're just listening to what the person is saying.

When I first started out, I only coached people over the phone. Most of my clients were local because I didn't use the Internet at all back then. Occasionally I would get referrals from other parts of the country. My clients now are from all over the world, and as you start to develop your marketing and build your business up, you'll definitely build it locally and internationally by using the power of the Internet.

Some coaches meet with clients twice per month, some every week. Sessions can be 20 minutes long or even 90 minutes. I meet with clients weekly for 30 minute sessions by phone.

CHAPTER 2
What Kinds of Coaches Are There?

As the industry advances, there are more and more different kinds of coaches. There are some areas that are easier to earn money in (business, sales, and executive coaching), and some are harder to earn money in (spirituality, creativity, life balance). Even though you may not be able to charge as much money, you can still earn a lot of money by having more clients, and by offering group coaching or selling products or programs.

Here are some of the specialties in the broad spectrum of the coaching profession:

- life coach

- health coach

- spiritual coach

- creativity coach

- life balance coach

- relationship coach

- business coach

- career coach

- leadership coach

- executive coach

One of the hottest coaching target markets or niches is **executive coaching**, working with top executives, CEOs, CFOs, and managers in corporations. Those tend to be the clients who pay the most for coaching. It's easy to see why these people pay the most since they make their companies lots of money.

Small business coaching is also very hot. That's where you would work with the owners of smaller-sized companies, and it's where I do most of my coaching. I got started as a generalist and then moved into small business coaching. There is a huge "mega-trend" toward people starting their own businesses making this a strong market.

Sales coaching is another hot niche market where you would help sales professionals increase their sales, multiply their commissions, and make more money. That would include real estate agents, financial advisors, all those who either have their own business or are fairly independent working in a company. It's not their own business because they may be a ReMax agent or a Windsor Capital Mortgage agent, but it is a lot like their own business and they want help growing their sales.

These are some of the hotter niches and good places to go and make lots of money. The reason they're hot is because it's very easy to financially justify the expense of coaching. If you can help a sales person increase their sales per month from $5,000 to $10,000 or from $10,000 to $20,000 or from $100,000 to $200,000—even if it's just from $140,000 to $160,000, that 5% increase can be huge.

Now, when it comes to **life coaching**, there are specific areas like **spiritual coaching, relationship coaching** or **coaching for retirees or men or women** and other niche markets. If you're a relationship coach, I recommend you be even more specific—you work with couples who are in relationships that aren't working or having problems, or you work with singles. The more specific you can be the better.

Career coaching would be somewhere between the executive and small-business coaching. Again, it ties in to making money. Although, sometimes people get career coaching and it's not necessarily because they want to make more money. There's also **creativity coaching, life balance coaching**, and niches like that.

I'm not sure how lucrative those are, but how do you pick? That's a key question when you're just starting out as a coach! A couple of things to consider are: (1) what are your drawn to, (2) what's your background, and (3) what is your intuition telling you? It's okay to start as a generalist and work towards a niche later. It took me a long while to go from generalist to small business coaching. I actually went to business coaching first and that's pretty broad too. You can go from business coaching to working with carpet- cleaning companies or web-development companies. I was in really broad business and sales coaching, and eventually got rid of the sales and focused only on small business coaching. And for many years now I've focused on helping coaches, which is an even more specific market!

These are some of the types of coaches. **You may choose to pick a specialty and become a certain type of coach**, and from a business standpoint it's really great when you work with certain groups of people. It's also easier to market yourself as one specific type of coach than it is to market yourself as all things to all people. That being said, even though I started off as a generalist coach, I got six clients my first month. You can start as a generalist if you want. Then, you don't have to make that decision up front. Once you have a niche it's so much easier to market, but you can get clients and get revenue without having a niche. It's a great way to get experience and work with a variety of people and let your niche come to you.

After years of coaching, however, **I would recommend focusing on one specialty, one group of people—your "target market" or niche**. I think it's a very smart move for any coach to choose a focus. For marketing purposes if for no other reason, you want to focus on one group. You will build more of a reputation that way as well.

This decision isn't always easy for most coaches, because they would like to coach anyone who comes to them. They don't understand why they should "narrow down" who they work with. If you try to be all things to all people, you usually end up being nothing to anyone.

You might start with a group of people you already know a lot about. Maybe you used to be a teacher or realtor—start with a profession that you have experience in. Or choose an area you are attracted to or feel highly competent in. Your confidence will attract more clients.

Now that doesn't mean you may not coach in more than one area. You might move from being a life coach to a relationship coach. You might move from being a relationship coach to coaching single men over 65 or recently divorced men getting back into dating—you could get really specific.

As an example, **I was a small business coach,** coaching small business owners to have fantastic lives on top of having a thriving business. Even though I was marketing myself as a small business coach, as soon as someone had a free session with me, I'd start asking them: if we get your business to where you want it to be, what will that do for your personal life? Are there some things in your personal life you want to change? Because I'll be coaching you not only on your business, but I want to make sure you don't just make a lot of money, but you create the life and the happiness you want and what really matters to you.

When we start talking about those things, some business owners love it and want lots of life coaching, while others might only want it at certain times when a situation comes up where they need help. Like, oh my gosh, my wife is freaking out and I need your help! You can absolutely coach people on more than one thing—I can't emphasize that enough.

One reason people have difficulty picking a target market is because they feel they will eliminate potential clients and limit themselves. But think about this for a second; even if you're a really successful coach, you're going to be coaching less than 30 people one-on-one. Even if you're doing group coaching and you're crazily successful, you might have 500 people in programs in a given year. If you charge only $500 a month for coaching, think about that—you don't need tons and tons of clients. Choosing a niche makes sense.

Everybody can benefit from coaching, but the more you can specialize, the better. If you're a business coach, you could coach realtors, mortgage brokers, financial planners, carpet cleaning businesses, or private investigators. I've actually worked with all of those. Definitely, the more you specialize the easier it is to get clients.

When you make a decision to become a coach, I want you to succeed. Now some do and some don't, some will and some won't. Some people, no matter how much I could teach them, or no matter how much I could coach them, may just never get there. But if you're determined and you're passionate about it, there's no stopping you.

Just turn on that little part of your brain that is absolutely determined, and you will become successful. I want to make it as easy as possible for you to become successful by sharing these ideas, not only in coaching terms, but in real world business terms, marketing terms, etc. I want to make sure that everybody is on the right path right from the beginning.

CHAPTER 3
What Certification Is Required to Become a Coach?

Q: Do you need to get certified as a professional coach in order to begin coaching?

A: No! You can start coaching today with zero training, no certifications, or anything else required (you don't even need a high school education)!

There is no regulation in the coaching industry, and you can start your own coaching business today with virtually zero requirements. There are no laws requiring certification in any of the 50 states in the US (although there may be other requirements; check with your local government to be sure). Why do some people get certified anyway? They are indoctrinated by coaching organizations and coaching schools to believe it's essential. A lot of coaching schools and coaching associations will certify you.

I've never had a potential client ask me if I was certified. The only ones who ever ask me are other coaches. It seems there's this secret system for how to help coaches get clients, and some of these certifying organizations say the only way for you to become certified is to hire a coach to mentor you who is already certified. It's like a little brotherhood of let's make sure we all keep making money. Become certified, and then you'll get hired by other coaches who want to become certified. I don't buy into that whole thing! Not all certifying organizations do this, but it's actually common.

Q: What is certification good for and why do people get it? A: To find out if you're good enough to be a coach–sort of.

Many people get certified so they can know they are a good coach (or at least they will be led to believe they are good). It's possible to be certified and not be that good, or to not be certified and be very, very good. I see myself as falling into the latter category. I'm not certified. And I'm darn good!

There's nothing wrong with certification, per se. If you go to one of the coaching schools that are connected to a certifying organization, take all the classes, and pass all the tests, there's a good chance you'll be a solid coach. But, there are no guarantees. It's a long and potentially expensive process. And if you want to get into the game quickly, getting certified can slow you down (and hold your coaching income hostage) and keep you from helping people right now!

Q: Where can you get certified? A: By anyone with a printer!

The truth is anyone can create a "certification" and many schools certify coaches. But, are they schools accredited through any governing body? There are a few coaching organizations that certify coaches. Two of the largest ones are ICF and IAC. I actually sat on the Board of Directors for the IAC for two years (and I wasn't certified and I'm still not). The ICF is the biggest organization with over 20,000 paying members. The IAC has 13,000 members. There's a lot of bureaucracy in these organizations. They have good intentions, but they also have "agendas" of their own.

I wasn't happy with what these associations were failing to offer their members, so I created a new association in 2012 and we already have over 4,000 founding members. www.ImpactForCoaches.com

Note: Most people within the coaching industry will tell you that you need to focus on getting certified through ICF. But that may or may not be right for you.

Q: Do clients care if you're certified?

A: No! (At least that's been my experience over more than a decade.)

Not one potential client has ever asked me if I was certified! Not one! Most clients only need to believe you can help them. Being certified might help potential clients to believe in you. But, not all that much, really. Remember that people hire you for themselves; they don't hire you for you. Partly they hire you for you, but ultimately they hire you for themselves, so when it comes to getting certified, it's not that important. If the potential client is in a situation where they have something they want, they're not getting it on their own yet, they're no longer willing to stay where they are, and they feel certain you can help them—boom, they will hire you and it doesn't matter if you're certified. Most people don't even know that coaches could be certified or what a certification would mean anyway.

It still may be worthwhile to go through whatever training might be required to get certified. I'm not saying there's no value in the process. All I'm saying is there's no need for it in today's economy. There's nothing that says you need to get some kind of a coaching certification.

Here is an article I wrote a few years ago called "The Dangers of Certification." It may answer more of your questions on certification.

"The Dangers of Certification"

After meeting the ICF President last month (that's the International Coaching Federation), I was all charged up about the idea of getting certified.

I'm not sure why. Perhaps I was excited to have people tell me how great I am. I could take a test and then have people say, "Yep, you are a top notch coach, Christian!" and feel all warm and fuzzy inside. But...

Then I thought about all of the clients that have ever hired me or had a free session with me (hundreds). Over the last seven years, guess how many have asked me if I was certified?

You may be shocked to find that the number is...ZERO!

In fact, the only people who have ever asked me if I was certified were other coaches. So why bother with certification?

Many coaches are spending a lot of time on getting certified. They want to make sure they are really great coaches. And, there's nothing wrong with that except...

Every second you spend on getting certified could be a second spent "getting clients"

or actually "working with clients."

There is nothing more important in your coaching business than actually coaching. I can't emphasize this enough. Why? Because this is where we make the biggest difference in the world, in people's lives, and in our own lives.

It breaks my heart to see hundreds, probably thousands of great coaches waiting to go out and get clients simply because they're waiting for their certification to feel good enough to get paid for their work.

For these people, certification isn't the issue, it's really about confidence. Some of us tend to get our sense of value from outside of ourselves. We need outside validation to know that we're really good enough. So...

Take this article as your official certificate of being a great coach. If you have a heart for coaching, I know you can make a great difference in people's lives. But, only if you actually coach people (and the other people in your coaching school don't count).

You've got to get out there and start getting clients. Spend less time getting ready to get clients (waiting for your website to be finished, for a brochure, business cards, or certification). Stop waiting and actually go out and get some clients!

The world needs you and your coaching... "Let's get people coached!"

CHAPTER 4

What Kind of Training and Skills Do You Need?

There are a lot of different types of coach training available, and you may decide you don't even need coach training. When I got started as a coach, I had already had my own professional coach for nine months and had gone through a lot of training through personal development seminars. I didn't have any specific "coach" training. I noticed I was already making a difference in people's lives, like with my friends and acquaintances. One birthday I had invited a bunch of friends over to my house to celebrate, and I asked everyone, instead of buying me a gift, to write down what impact I'd made on their life. That gave me a lot of confidence to feel like I really do make a difference in people's lives. Since I had my own coach, I felt like I knew what to do with people in coaching sessions and how to facilitate the coaching process.

You may or may not need coach training, and only you will know if you do. If you feel you'd like to be really good at coaching when you get started, if you'd like to have a little bit more understanding of how the flow of coaching sessions go and what to do in each session, then it would be a good idea to get coach training. And I think probably for everybody, you can always keep learning. I'm a lifelong learner, and I'm constantly training and learning new things, new techniques. I haven't actually joined a coaching school or graduated from a coaching school, but I've taken tons of training on coaching-related topics and coaching-related skills. I love to learn and I love to grow, so coach training is probably a good idea, if you're like me.

If you have some other kind of experience that leads you to be a great coach like having experience as a therapist, where you've been trained as a therapist and you've been doing therapy for a while, or you've been trained as a consultant and you've been consulting for a while—those kinds of experiences lend very well to coaching. Therefore, those kinds of people tend to be able to jump right into personal coaching quickly with little training.

Then there are the super achievers, those who have achieved a lot in their life, maybe started a business, grew it to a few million dollars and sold it. That kind of person also might not need a lot of training, because success in any one area of life can teach you a lot, and you can apply that to other areas. This life experience lends really well to becoming a coach and hitting the ground running.

It doesn't mean that if you don't have a background in therapy or consulting or you're not a super achiever, you can't be a great coach. Those are just situations where people tend to be able to get started as a coach with less training.

If you specifically wanted to coach a niche market, say business owners, you don't necessarily need training in how to coach business owners, but more of what I would call "market research" to understand what business owners need. If you have other skills like having been a therapist, for example, you could work well with business owners, because a lot of the biggest problems they have are in their head, so you might not want to get a lot more training for that. It's more about understanding the deeper psychology and doing research like interviewing some successful business owners and some struggling business owners and looking at what's going on in their head.

What's making the successful ones successful, and what's going on with the ones who aren't as successful? Then ask yourself: "How might I be able to help them if I were coaching these people?" Research sounds big and scary, but it's really about talking to a few people and asking a few questions of the ones who are doing well and those who aren't doing, as well and getting to know them and what makes them tick.

You may, however, need some training in the business side of coaching. You'll need to learn how to stage your marketing campaign to get clients, unless you get hired by a company that has internal coaches who work on staff.

I'm not against training in any shape or form; I have spent over $100,000 in different trainings over the years, some that applied to techniques in coaching, some that applied to business development, and some in personal development—so I'm a really big fan of training.

Beyond any formal training you may choose to take, these are some essential **skills required to be successful as a coach**:

- a love of helping people move beyond their challenges

- an interest in personal growth/personal development/self help

- a willingness to learn

- the ability to develop rapport

- a talent for influencing others

- confidence in yourself and your skills

- the ability to learn how to get clients (unless you get a job as a coach)

Although all these items are helpful, in terms of what you actually need to get started, there are basically only two things required to become a successful personal coach. **First, you need the confidence and know-how to be able to help people in the coaching process.** If you feel really confident and competent you can help people, you could probably get started with coaching right now. Of course, you need to know what to do in your coaching sessions. Having a process for facilitating your coaching is going to be useful. But when it comes down to the basics, confidence is on top.

Second you need to be able to get clients. That's really all that's required to become a coach. You actually don't have to *have* any kind of training. You don't *have* to have any kind of certification. Pretty much anybody can become a coach.

Now that said, anyone can call themselves a coach, but not necessarily everyone's going to be instantly a great coach, and not everyone's going to be able to get coaching clients. However, if you have the confidence that you can help people and the ability to get clients, that's honestly all you need. Certainly there are lots of coach trainings available and you can spend the rest of your life going through coach trainings if you want to. But it's absolutely not necessary to work as a coach.

The truth is you need to be able to do these things:

1. Connect with people

2. Put yourself in front of the people who have something they want to change, and also have a challenge making the changes and they can't stand being where they are any longer,

3. Show that you really understand what they are going through.

4. Demonstrate how you can help them

If you can do these things, there's no stopping you. You can be 25, 75, or any age. There are no limits in coaching. You simply need the desire and commitment. If you are committed to being successful and committed to making a difference with coaching, you will do well.

CHAPTER 5
How Do You Find the Right Coach Training for You?

If you decide you want extensive study and practice before you'll be ready to start coaching, you can review the different coaching schools you can find online. (See Resource section for a link). There are hundreds of coach training programs available, and I'm sure most of them are really good, so they're all worth looking into. Some of the **criteria you might want to look at are**:

- what are the class sizes?

- how many people are going to be in each class?

- are the classes live or are they just audio recordings?

- what is the overall philosophy of the coach training school?

- how long does it take to get through the training?

- how much does it cost?

Some coach training is more down-to-earth, some is more philosophical. A lot of coach trainings are very touchy-feely, personal growth oriented instead of achievement oriented. I believe in a more "results oriented" approach. Why? Because, being results oriented will necessitate personal growth. As your client achieves goals, they will have to grow personally, so the two are really connected.

Einstein said, "We can't solve problems by using the same kind of thinking we used when we created them." Achieving goals is the same, we have to learn more, become more, in order to accomplish a goal. We'll be tested and challenged and as a result we'll have to grow personally.

I don't necessarily feel like coaching should be only about personal growth, unless that's what somebody's hiring you for; but most people are going to be hiring your for a specific result they want to achieve in their life or business, so I would recommend looking for coaching schools that are rooted in real world principles, real world accomplishment. You may have to do a lot of digging to know for sure.

Another thing to look into is, how long will it take for you to graduate? Some coach training programs could take four years or longer to get through all the training, and there's nothing wrong with that. It just means it could slow down the process for how quickly you're able to start working with coaching clients. On the flip side, it may also be a super training with extensive, quality content.

Another consideration is, how long will it take before the trainers in the coaching program think you should be working with clients? For example, some coaching programs will have you start working with people right away. Others will say you've got to wait until you graduate, then wait until you get certified, and then you need to do a certain number of practice hours before they recommend you start working with clients. That's something else to look into.

Also, which program fits in best with your philosophy? My feeling is that the best way to learn anything is to practice it in the real world, so I want to start getting clients right away.

You might also be concerned with how much it costs. Definitely how much you pay for your coach training program is going to be based on your budget. Additionally, you'll want to know if they offer a money back guarantee. If they don't, then how confident are they in what they're doing? I don't feel safe enough to enroll in a program that doesn't offer a guarantee. I want to know for sure that what they offer is going to be a good fit for me, so I would make sure they offer a money back guarantee. You may not need to go through the whole program before you get your money back, but at least a good 30-day money back guarantee would offer you some security.

If you have a good background and experience and only want to learn some specific techniques rather than taking an entire course at a coaching school, you could just pick a couple of classes to fill in holes where you think you need certain skills and techniques. In addition, one of the best ways to learn coaching is to be coached by a really good coach. That's how I got started. You can go to coaches you've heard are good and learn from them. Being coached is also part of coaching, because you're always learning and you will continue to face your own personal challenges.

However, if you're hiring a coach just to learn about coaching or to learn how to grow your coaching business, it's a little bit of an unnatural process. If you hire a coach because you need a coach, then you're working on things because you really want something to change (versus you're going to be coached because you want to learn about coaching or how to grow your coaching business). I would examine for yourself if there are certain things you really want to change—whether it's losing weight and getting fit, or finding or improving your relationship, or getting more in touch with your spirituality—anything you want to change. Then, if there is something like that, I would look at hiring a coach for yourself as a good first step. And you can observe the process as you are being coached.

I also have my own coach training program. I created this program so that other coaches can learn the methodologies that I've been using to help my clients get great results. To find out more about it, go to http://www.RapidCoachingAcademy.com

CHAPTER 6
How Much Do Coaches Get Paid?

One of the things I love about coaching is that **coaches get paid a lot—** even the coaches who don't charge a lot. Average coaching fees are about $300 a month for three 45-minute sessions. Fees are dependent on how long the coach has been coaching, how extensive their knowledge is, and what other coaches are charging. Even $300 a month seems a small amount to charge for coaching, but $300 a month for three 45-minute sessions is $133 per hour. That's pretty good money. One of my coach training clients grew his business from zero to six figures in 90 days and he's charging over $2,000 a month for coaching small business owners.

Now, the average starting life coaching fee is around $300 a month, but I know of life coaches charging $800 a month and they have plenty of clients. The range for small business coaching averages $600 a month and ranges anywhere between $400 and $2,000 a month, maybe even more. I know one coach who charges $25,000 a year and gets paid for the whole year. Executive coaches who coach executives in corporations and large companies can get paid anywhere between $10,000 per year to over $200,000 per client per year. Even if you're only charging $195 a month for four 30-minute sessions, which is basically a session a week, that's still decent money at $97.50 an hour.

At some point you may want to raise your fees, although I almost never raise my fees to existing clients. How I raise my rates is with new clients. In general, clients don't stick around forever; they get on the right track and know where they want to go and take off. When you're starting out, I would say it might be better to be flexible. On the flip side,

I know a lot of coaches aren't doing a good job of showing how what they do will help someone, and that's when money becomes an issue. If you get people really clear and excited about what they want, and show them how what they're currently doing is not achieving those goals, then there's a good likelihood they will hire you no matter what you're charging, if it's reasonable.

How much should *you* charge or how much should coaches get paid? Some coaches charge by the hour. You just call up, set a day and time, and you have one coaching session. You may never have another one, or you may have one here and another there. I highly recommend not doing that. I want to get you off on the right foot and that is, you want to set a monthly fee for coaching, and you want to have a set number of sessions you offer, whether it's three 45-minute sessions or four half-hour sessions or three half-hour sessions or two to three one-hour sessions.

However you structure it, you'll need to test it out and get a feel for what works best. Some people feel that in a half hour they can't get enough done, but I feel like a half hour is plenty.

I also recommend that you sign up clients for at least six months at a time. This will allow them to really see the results that coaching helps them achieve! And it means that you don't have to keep coaching new clients and then waiting for them to decide if they are going to continue with you the next month. It's better for both of you when you agree to a six month (or longer) coaching relationship right from the start.

That's how much coaches charge. **But how much do coaches actually earn?** Certainly there's no limit to how much coaches can earn. Some coaches are making a million dollars a year or more from their coaching, and some are making $10,000 a year or $20,000 a year doing it part time or attempting to do it full time, but are having a hard time with getting coaching clients, which is obviously an important piece of the puzzle.

I was interviewed by *Forbes Magazine* for an article a few years ago. It was about surprising six-figure jobs, and professional coaching was listed as one of them. The article mentioned that at that time there were about 10,000 coaches worldwide, however, that was a huge mistake. Actually there were at least 10,000 members of several different coaching associations, the two biggest being ICF and IAC. But those members were (and continue to be) tiny fractions of the actual numbers of people out in the world who call themselves a coach.

My estimate is that there are about 300,000 coaches today—people either working as a coach or working on becoming a coach. Or they've become a coach, and they're working on getting more clients. At wherever stage of the game, I'd say there are about 300,000. That's just my personal ballpark estimate based on a lot of different factors. You really can't find any hard data on the actual numbers, but I know there are way more than 10,000 coaches.

Besides the fees and quantity of coaches, another issue is longevity. I'm not sure what the average length of a coaching career is. A lot of people get started and get trained, and then never really get going. Some start and give up and some never ever give up; ultimately it's life circumstances that make it harder for some people than others.

I was talking to another leader in the coaching industry, and she said a lot of coaches are getting a regular day job and then using their coaching skills within their job. There's nothing wrong with that. I feel that it's not necessarily a waste, but there are so many hungry people who would hire a coach today if the right coach was in front of them, approaching them, marketing to them the right way, connecting with them and building a relationship with them in the ways that I teach.

When I started in coaching, I was $72,000 in debt from a previous business and had almost no financial resources to get started. I had to scrape and claw and bootstrap my way up and nothing was going to stop me. Once I started getting paid good money for coaching—having people pay me $500, $600 a month or $250 an hour, I could never go back and get some part- time job where I'm making $10 to $20 an hour. There was no turning back and I loved it. Not only was I getting paid a lot, I really loved coaching. It was fun and rewarding to watch my clients grow. I loved getting e-mails or phone calls saying, "I was working on this situation that you coached me on and it turned out great!" In the beginning I was able to eke out a modest living my first three years, and over time my income grew slowly and steadily, eventually to six figures and beyond.

CHAPTER 7
Where Can You Get a Coaching Job?

Businesses love coaching and I would imagine that at least half of all coaching—if not more—is purchased by businesses of some sort. Small businesses, large businesses, all types of businesses hire coaches. And certainly there are lots of people who hire personal life coaches, relationship coaches, etc.

But if you're looking for security, you may want to investigate getting a job as a coach within an organization. I recently got an e-mail from a friend who had information on a job offer from a financial services company in Dallas that was looking for a coach to coach their employees, and it was paying between $60,000 and $90,000 a year plus bonuses. When I was first starting out as a coach, I would have jumped on that in a heartbeat. I'd have thought, "Oh gosh, I can have a solid steady income and get paid as a coach and do what I love? Hallelujah!" I would have been all over that.

Now, however, over a decade later, making the kind of money I'm making these days, having the freedom and flexibility I have - that kind of offer wouldn't even appeal to me. But there are those kinds of jobs as coaches in traditional companies. I remember being at a coach training, and a coach there told me he was working as a coach in a company, so there definitely are coaching jobs available, but they tend to be a bit harder to find, especially based on the number of coaches in the world.

Some companies hire a staff coach. I believe that's going to be a growing trend. It's easier to pay somebody $60,000 a year to be on staff as a coach than it is to pay an independent coach $300 or $500 a month per employee. There will likely be more and more coaching jobs becoming available.

Check online job postings and classified ads through coaching networks, coaching organizations, and coach training companies. You can also check through online job sites like http://www.monster.com. Keep yourself in the loop through staying in the sphere of influence of other coaches, organizations, and people like me.

I also created a service for coaches that can help you find a great job as a coach. Go to **http://www.JobListingsForCoaches.com** to check it out.

Sometimes a very successful coach will hire other coaches to work for them, so although it's not a big company, it would be steady work and you wouldn't have to find your own clients or do your own administration. That being said, the majority of those who become coaches start their own coaching businesses.

CHAPTER 8
Do You Need to Get Your Own Clients?

Yes! About 90% of all coaches have a business and need to get their own clients. Where do you find them? All over the place—I have clients around the world—in Italy, Australia, England, Spain, Germany, Brazil, Canada and throughout the USA.

You can start out by asking anyone you know or meet if they know anyone who might want to get coaching and have a free session with you. You might also call or send an email to friends, acquaintances, associates, people you hang out with. Let them know you're getting involved in coaching and tell them a little bit about it. You can say, "I'm just getting started so I'm not charging much at all. If you're interested or know someone who might be interested, the first session is free, so you can try it out before you would have to pay anything."

That might be an easy way to step out there, especially since you may be in a place where you're not ready to pick a niche right away—and that's okay. I think sometimes coaches try to pick their niche too soon, but when it comes to marketing and getting clients, it's kind of like a Catch-22. It's a great thing as a coach to be a generalist and work with a wide variety of people so you can see who you like working with and how people respond to your coaching, but on the flip side, once you have a target market then your marketing can take off.

You might want to start attending your local Chamber of Commerce meetings or a networking group meeting. There are several good groups out there such as BNI and other business networking groups. Or maybe volunteer in a place where it's a very social setting—anywhere you can get around other people and talk about what you do.

Most of my clients in the early days came locally from giving talks. I was asked to speak everywhere. I was pretty comfortable speaking, but if you're afraid of public speaking and you don't like it, you don't have to do it and you can still be successful. I would, however, recommend learning to like it. Doing public speaking isn't essential, but it makes it easier and better to grow your business faster. These days, I hardly do any public speaking at all, not like I did in the beginning.

If you do teleclasses, that can be just as good and in some ways, even better, because you can reach people from around the world. Now if you're just not a fan of speaking, you can grow your coaching business through writing articles and eBooks. And if you can't write, you can hire a writer or trade with one for coaching.

If you aren't comfortable speaking in public, I recommend you join Toastmasters (http://www.toastmasters.org) and become more confident and competent in your speaking. You don't have to become a great speaker, just comfortable enough to make a positive impression. One of my best friends is a professional speaker, and he's a really polished storyteller and very entertaining. That's just not me; that's not my style. I used to say all the stuff you're not supposed to say as a public speaker, but I didn't worry about that. I just focused on serving, supporting, teaching, imparting knowledge, inspiring people, and sharing ideas. I don't consider myself a public speaker as much as a teacher and I can definitely teach.

Nevertheless, I got my first six clients after giving a talk at a Toastmasters semi-annual conference. I talked on motivation and what motivates people. I think it was called "Motivating From Within." I had about 30 people in the room and offered them all a free coaching session. About 12 took me up on it, and out of those 12, I got three coaching clients. Then I did that same talk to about 40 people at a Chamber of Commerce in my area. Again, I offered a free session, and I might have had 12 people sign up for the free session and got another three clients out of that.

I got six clients right away, just from giving talks and offering free sessions. At that time I wasn't even doing the free sessions anywhere near the way I do them now. These days a much higher percentage of people sign up for coaching from my free session process.

I did some of the same elements back then, but not all of them. In fact, my free sessions lasted much longer back then, and I didn't get as many clients from them, but it worked to a degree. When you're first starting out you may want to do your free sessions in person. The percentage of people hiring you will go up a little by doing them in person. When you get busier, and you're getting a lot of people wanting free sessions, I would say do them over the phone for sure.

It's unfortunate that many techniques are taught to people on how to grow their coaching business that absolutely don't work or they work poorly, so the coach thinks maybe these people aren't hiring me because I'm not a good enough coach. You're told as a coach that when you do these things, they are supposed to work, yet they don't work and they lead you to start doubting yourself. I went through this in the early days, having to learn what worked well through trial and error. I have tested just about every marketing method out there.

A lot of coaches are taught to get clients by offering a free coaching session. I do recommend this, but not to do it as a sample of coaching - which is what most people say to do. People will get a taste and they'll want it, like Mrs. Field's chocolate chip cookies. But cookies and coaching aren't the same and this doesn't work that way.

Giving a free sample of coaching can work occasionally, but it doesn't work every time you coach somebody. The worst thing is that if they don't hire you, and this happens over and over, you could start thinking, "Wow, does anybody ever really hire a coach?" Or you think, "Maybe I'm just not a good enough coach." You go back and get more and more coach training. You have no idea how many coaches are trained beyond surgeons, and are still not getting clients. **It comes down to confidence and knowing HOW to get clients,** and if you can master those two ingredients, there is no reason anyone would ever drop out of coaching.

In one of my programs I spend four hours teaching how to do free sessions that aren't simply a sample of coaching. It's called "Free Sessions That Sell: the Client Enrollment System". It's a clinic on all I've ever learned about sales training, and I apply it specifically to the process of getting clients. I've developed it into a system that creates tremendous value for potential clients and gets people to the point where they see how coaching helps them so they would want to hire a coach.

Of course not everybody's going to hire a coach no matter what you do, but this works like nothing else I've ever seen, and I have studied other people's programs and what other people teach. This is the cream of the crop. Again, the name of the program is "Free Sessions that Sell: The Client Enrollment System" and you can check it out at http://www. freesessionsthatsell.com.

The program goes into how to find out what's going on in someone's head, what they really want, what their challenges are, and how to show them that you'll help them get the results they want. That's why they'll hire you, so that's a really important piece of the puzzle. There's so much depth to what I teach, but it's not hard to learn. I'm not keeping secrets. I want to serve people through everything I do, so even my marketing serves people.

Every piece of marketing I do can make a difference in people's lives. Of course a lot of people are going to buy the program, but I want even the few people who never buy, to be helped. Certainly I want to make money with my programs and products, but even people who don't buy anything send me e-mails saying, "I went to your website/read your emails and I didn't buy your program, but I learned a lot. I was on the phone with a prospect, and I felt more confident and certain about what I was doing, and I got the client."

You can use your marketing process in such a way that you really serve and support people and develop a relationship with them by serving them over and over. And then when they are stuck or something comes up that makes them feel like they need help right now, you're the one at the top of their mind. You're the one they think of and they want to hire you, or maybe you just give them an offer for a free session, and they have that free session, because they know you and they see the value in it. Then boom, they hire you!

In terms of how fast you can make your coaching business successful, it will depend on some of the skills you already have. If you are comfortable with public speaking, if you're a good writer, if you can find your way around the Internet, if you can develop your own website and are pretty tech savvy, you could grow your business pretty quickly. If you don't have those skills, it doesn't mean you're not going to grow your business, but you may have a longer ramp up time.

There are just so many ways you can grow your coaching business, which, in a nutshell are: writing articles, speaking, networking, and the Internet. It comes down to basically these four methods. You don't have to do all four. Some people never speak or some people only speak. When I first started out, I did a lot of public speaking and networking—I didn't use the Internet at all, and I hated to write, so I didn't write. When I decided to start writing and using the Internet, my business grew even faster. There are a lot of coaches who have gone through four years of coach training and are certified and they still don't have clients...because they are not marketing themselves.

If you feel like you're ready to start coaching people and you don't feel like you need any coach training, then what I recommend is **start learning how to go out and get clients.** If you're determined to make it happen, you'll make it happen. If you love coaching, you'll find a way to get clients. If you present coaching as a service with tangible results that's an investment in the person or their business, you will win them over.

The main thing is that you learn to do free coaching sessions the way I teach them. Once you have a free coaching session with a prospect and you show them the way to awaken what they want for their life or business, and it helps to uncover the biggest challenges, and you can show them what you do as a coach will help them get what they want and overcome their challenges, then you can sell coaching.

There's nothing better in the world than being a personal coach, making a difference in people's lives, getting paid well, and having freedom and flexibility. Once you get a taste of it, I don't know how anybody can let it go. The biggest obstacles that hold people back from being successful are their inner demons, their self doubt. That, and not knowing how to effectively get clients and sign them up for coaching. Master confidence and marketing and you're in!

CHAPTER 9
How Do You Start Your Own Business?

It sounds rather simplistic, but in order to start your own coaching business, **you really don't need anything except the ability to take payments**. Checks work, but credit cards are even better. It definitely makes sense to have your own website, and having a shopping cart system that works with your website allows people to purchase your products and services with credit cards. You might want to get a combination shopping cart/database organizer like the one I use called http://www.carts-forcoaches.com. They have a sister company which does the credit card processing, and I use both of these companies.

You may need a business license, so check with your city offices or Chamber of Commerce. I didn't have business cards or a website before I started my business; it took me two years before I had a website. My client who took his business from zero to six figures in 90 days had business cards he printed out on his printer. You can also get fairly nice-looking ones for free at http://www.vistaprint.com.

Some coaches decide to become incorporated. My business is incorporated, because I had started a different business first. I took the corporation I already had and I said, "Okay, now we're a coaching and training company instead of a gift business." You don't necessarily need legal advice to get incorporated. You could become an LLC (Limited Liability Corporation) or just be a sole proprietor. If you're not sure what you want to do, accountants and attorneys have the best advice on those issues. Mostly they would be concerned about protecting your assets and tax matters. It's a good idea to incorporate or to have an LLC for tax purposes so you end up keeping more money because of what you can write off. You might also want to become a separate corporate entity so you can protect yourself from lawsuits where they can only go after the corporation and not the individual.

You can get incorporated online for around $150. If you prefer, you can find an attorney who may charge around $600-$800. Some may even charge a couple thousand dollars. You need to look online for the domain name you want to incorporate, and if it doesn't exist you can buy it. I use a service called www.namecheap.com; it's less than $10 to buy your website name and you can search to see if any of the names you want are open and available. That was another thing my attorney did for me; I came up with the name of the company before I bought my website name and then did a domain search.

You may also want to get business liability insurance for protection in case someone sues you. I've not actually heard of any coaches getting sued, but I'm sure it's probably happened. I have never had business liability insurance, but it's something that is a good idea. Check with an insurance agent for the best advice, and ask some other coaches. I think it's between $300 and $800 per year to get covered in this way, and it's up to $1 million or $10 million coverage.

CHAPTER 10
What Are the Start-Up Costs?

Start-up costs vary from zero to several thousand dollars, depending on your budget. If you decide to pursue that path, **coach training** could vary from between $500 to $14,000 or more depending on where you train and how much training you need. This depends on your personal preference and your previous experience and education. The most expensive one I know of is $20,000, but there could definitely be some that are even more expensive.

Some new coaches have a background in business, sales, or marketing and don't need a ton of **business and sales training**, but you'll probably still need some because a coaching business is different than other types of businesses. I would say between $500 and $10,000 for business, marketing, and sales training, depending on where you train and how much you need to learn.

When I started my coaching business, I didn't have a big budget (because I was $70,000 in debt from a previous business start-up) so I actually had to learn a lot about how to get clients from trial and error. This is the harder, slower way to grow a coaching business. As I started to bring in income, a lot of my financial outlay went to learning how to market, sell, and get clients. I felt that was the best investment for me to grow a successful business.

I have a training program, which teaches everything you need to know about sales and marketing for your coaching business, and gives you a ton of 'done for you' materials for under $5,000. Of course I think it's the best program on the market! It's called "Client Attraction and

Money Making Mastery". It's a complete training program on how to build your coaching business quickly! You can find out more about it by visiting: **http://www.clientattractionandmoneymakingmastery.com**

Some other business costs include putting up your website, getting business cards, setting up credit card processing, as well as any technology you need and the standard office supplies. You might want to get a separate phone line, depending on your living situation and if you have a family. These days, phone lines and cell phones are becoming less and less expensive, and there are unlimited long distance plans for one monthly price.

Since I do most of my coaching over the phone, I think a separate phone line is a good idea. Almost all coaching is done over the phone initially, although I have had sessions with people in person. There are some techniques that are better to do in person than over the phone. In general though, 90 to 95% of all the coaching sessions I've ever had has been over the phone, right from the beginning.

To save money, you can create your website yourself, you can get free business cards, and you can make do with what you have technology- wise until you can update it. In the beginning, I used to do most of my web stuff myself. Then I got to the point where I was successful enough to hire someone do a website for my coaching business. But if you have a decent budget, it's great to outsource as much as you can, so having somebody do your website for you is fantastic. I now have a full team of people working in my business including a few virtual assistants (VAs) who do a lot of minor updates and administrative projects, which allows me to be able to create products and programs live right on the web.

If you pay for your website, business cards, etc., you'll spend between $900 and $6,500 for typical business start-up costs. I know that's a pretty big range, since people charge all different prices from $500 to $5,000 for a website. You could consider going to http://www.elance. com, where you can find a lot of low cost services to get your business going at whatever range of budget you have in mind.

If you have a bigger start up budget, you can ramp up faster. If you have a small budget, you can still have a lucrative career as a coach, it just may take a bit longer.

CHAPTER 11
Why Do People Buy Coaching?

There are four elements that will lead people to hire you as a coach. One reason is because there's **something they want that they don't have**. Here are some examples:

- a salesperson who wants to increase her sales commissions and needs to improve her technique or confidence

- a man who wants to start a business

- a woman who wants to grow her business

- a man who wants to find a career that lights him up

- a single woman who wants to get into a relationship

- someone who wants to lose weight

Element number one is that there's something they want that they don't have now. It could be internal or external. Some people want peace of mind, some want to get back in touch with their spirituality, and some want certain internal qualities. But most are looking for something external.

The truth is most people want something they don't have but a lot of them are small wants, or if they're big wants they don't want them that badly. For example, maybe they would like to get into a relationship but they're ok being single, or they would like to start a business but they get paid well and the job they are in now isn't so bad.

The second element is that they're **having a hard time getting what they want on their own**. They want a different job, but they don't know what kind of job they want, or they want to start a business, but they don't know how to start a business, or they want to grow their business but they've been trying for a year and a half and they're stuck at the same income level that they were for the last year and a half so something's not working. They can't get there on their own or it's not happening fast enough, so maybe the business is growing but too slowly, or they're starting to get more dates but still not meeting the right people. Because if they are getting their desired result on their own, there wouldn't be a need to get a coach, right? It's either not happening or not happening fast enough.

The third condition that needs to be present for somebody to hire a coach is that something is uncomfortable—there's a reason why **they can't stay where they are**. If they stay where they are it's too painful and they don't want to continue with the status quo. Maybe they hate their job and they're about ready to quit, but they need to make money somehow, so they're not going to quit yet. They might hire a career coach. Suppose it's a salesperson and they're making some money but not enough, and they have to dip into savings every month, or compared to the other salespeople they're at the bottom of the pack. Even though they're making good money, they might want it for pride purposes. They can't stand being towards the bottom or maybe they're super competitive.

Possibly a single person who wants to get into a relationship is feeling lonely, and for three years they've been dating a lot but just can't get into a relationship. For some reason it doesn't stick and they want it so badly, because they can't stand being alone and not having a date every Friday night or someone to spend weekends with. There has to be some pain—and the desire of something they want. They can't stay where they are any longer.

The fourth aspect that has to happen in order for someone to want to hire a coach is that they **feel certain you can help them**. In order for somebody to look for and hire a coach they need to be open to hiring a coach.

People who have all four of these things happening are going to hire you fairly easily, endlessly, and constantly, and that's why it's good to become one certain type of a coach. Because if you become a relationship coach, you might be teaching people tips about how to get in a relationship, and they will get to know you as they're learning from you. Then eventually they will get to the point where they can't stand being where they are any longer and they want your help. They've been learning from you and some of the things are working but not fast enough.

Recap: People hire a coach because...

A. They want something.

B. They aren't getting it on their own (at least not fast enough).

C. They can't stand being where they are any longer.

D. They feel certain you can help them.

Here is an article I wrote a while ago covering why people hire a coach and the traits of successful coaches.

Ideal Coaching Age | Finding Clients | Traits of Successful Coaches

You may not be one of "them," but you'll still discover a lot about how to find new coaching clients from what I'm about to share with you. I'm going to tell you a little known "secret" about why people hire coaches (and it's not something you'll learn anywhere else). This secret will revolutionize the way you think about finding new coaching clients (in a very good way)!

Before I share this with you, I need to address something. A lot of people have been writing in to get my opinion on some things:

--> "How young is too young to get started as a personal coach?" or...

--> "Am I too 'old' to get started in personal coaching?" Now...

Even if yu're not one of "these people," my answer to this question about "age" will still apply to you because there's a bigger, deeper, more universal principle that I'm going to explain. And...

If you ARE one of the people wondering if you're too young or too old to be a coach, what you're really wondering is "will people hire me?" If you have doubts, fears, or limiting beliefs about making it as a coach, this may be some of your "inner work."

You may need to address this stuff within yourself. And perhaps I can help you. But, for now I want to take a different approach and share with you...

**** Why does anyone hire a coach anyway? *****

The answer to this question will shed light on the "mystery that is coaching" and will clear up the whole "age issue" once and for all. And, when you understand what I'm about to share, it will (hopefully) forever change the way you go about getting coaching clients.

There are actually 3 answers to this question, each one "deeper" and more true than the last! Here's the first one...

1. People hire a coach because they want something. Here are some sample reasons people hire a coach:

   • A sales professional wants to increase her sales numbers.

   • A single man wants to find his soul mate.

   • An executive wants to grow the company and get more public kudos.

   • A middle manager wants to find his dream career.

   • A small business owner wants to take more vacations.

   • An aging man wants to get back in shape. But...

Even though people want something, it's not enough to make them hire a coach. Lots of people want something, but never hire a coach.

So why do people hire a coach?

2. People can't stay where they are any longer. Not only do they want something, they can no longer settle for the status quo. If we look more closely at the examples from above, we'll find that these people have something deeper going on:

- A sales professional can't cover her bills each month, is dipping into her savings, and needs to make more money fast or she'll end up losing everything.

- A single man has been lonely for 5 years and knows he's afraid to ask out women he finds attractive.

- An executive can't get his team to take the initiative and his board of directors are breathing down his neck.

- A middle manager is bored with his job and can't take another year doing this meaningless job.

- A small business owner works 80 hours a week and feels like a slave to her business.

- An aging man is feeling "old", starts to realize that some of his friends haven't lasted this long and if he doesn't clean up his act he may not have much longer either. And...

This may make them start looking for a solution to their problems, and perhaps to start looking for a coach. But, this may not be enough for them to hire you.

3. People will hire YOU based on how well you can create certainty that you can help them. They need to feel sure that coaching will work, and that it will work for them. And here's how you can do that (at any age).

How To Create Certainty That You Can Help

1. Teaching solutions to some of their challenges creates certainty that you can help them. You can write an article for business owners on how to be more focused, delegate more, etc., or share secrets for single men to meet women.

When you teach something valuable to the people you want to coach, they will see you as an expert, a person who really knows his stuff! This will help potential clients begin to consider you as the "home-run" solution they're looking for. They'll think, "If he knows this much about X, then if he worked with me personally, I wonder what would happen."

2. People will hire you based on how well you demonstrate "you understand them" (and their situation) above almost all else. If you can explain the "ins and outs" of the situation they are in a few things happen.

    People will believe that they are not alone. They aren't the only ones going through this (most people think they are the first one to have the problem that they have). They will obviously see you as an expert at handling this kind of thing because you know it and understand it so well.

    They will feel a connection to you. People feel a sense of rapport or connection with people they have something in common with. When you show you understand them, they feel that sense of commonality. This will be a BIG factor in making them want to hire you. You can demonstrate how well you understand them by discussing what their situation must feel like, how it shows up in their daily lives, and perhaps how their problems came to be.

3. Offer a satisfaction guarantee on your coaching. I don't guarantee results because 90% of clients' results depend on the clients themselves (how much effort they put in, how much they follow through, etc.).

    I tell them that after the first month, if they don't see that the work we're doing is going to make the difference they are looking for, or if they aren't happy for any reason, we can stop working together and they can have a full refund.

    I call it my "unconditional happiness guarantee." It makes them feel "safer" about giving coaching a try AND it shows how confident you are in the work you do. When you offer a guarantee it shows you mean business!

Bottom Line

I know coaches who were successful at age 19 (I started when I was 24)! I know coaches who are in their "later years" and are doing very well in coaching too. Ultimately, your success depends mainly on your ability to understand your clients' needs, connect with them, and show them that you can help them. If you can do this, you'll be successful in coaching at any age.

COACHING TIPS: "Traits of Successful Coaches"

Here's a list of traits that coaches who are successful in coaching all seem to possess (in no particular order):

- A strong desire to help people

- Confidence in themselves (although we all have our insecurities)

- Determination

- Great communication skills

- A love of learning, especially learning about people

- An inner drive

- Feeling "guided" by a higher power or their intuition

Do you posses some of these traits? If so, then I have a feeling you're going to achieve a lot of success as a professional coach. Still... There are few "overnight successes" in life. True success takes time. Although one of my clients started and grew his coaching business to over six figures in just 90 days, this is by far an exception.

If you don't have a lot of the traits mentioned above, it may be time to do some of your own personal growth work to develop these aspects of yourself, because anyone can get better at anything! And if you really want to be a success in the coaching world, I know you can do it!

CHAPTER 12
Who Hires a Coach?

All kinds of people hire coaches. My clients have ranged in age from early 20s to mid 60s. They're normal people, people like you and me. I hired a coach when my whole life was a mess. I'd started a business that wasn't going anywhere. I was in a relationship that I wasn't happy in. I was out of shape and in a job I hated. I had all of those pains, so I was seeking a coach. I was looking to find a coach to help me. There are people looking for a coach right now, because enough things aren't working for them and they want some help turning their life around.

Now, there are going to be other people who would never think, "I want a coach." Maybe you'll get to know them or they'll get to know you, and you'll be developing a relationship with them either through writing articles or giving talks. You may offer them a free session, and if you do it in a powerful way, those people who wouldn't have thought of hiring a coach will hire you.

There are people all over the place who hire coaches. You'd be surprised that people you might already know, people at your former jobs, your neighbors, your service providers at the bank, dentist's office—they are all hiring coaches! Not that it's a big secret, but some people don't think to mention it. And it is happening more and more. There are coaches out there and there are people hungry for coaching—some who have never even heard of coaching. And if they heard of it and saw how coaching could help them, they would hire a coach right now.

It's a shame that there are all these coaches who are trained and aren't getting clients, just because they don't know how to market themselves, and all these people who need coaching are suffering because some coaches are giving up. But coaching makes a huge difference in people's lives, so don't give up! Coaching is one of the best things you can do. My mantra is "let's get people coached." There's nothing I could be more grateful for in my life than this thing called coaching. As a client, it's changed my life ten times over, and as a coach, it's the most rewarding thing I've ever done for work—and it pays very well. It's a miracle in my life and I really want it for all of you.

Years ago, I had a coaching client who was a salesperson, and she called and left an excited message on my voice mail that said, "After our coaching call today, I called a prospect who said he already had someone he was working with but thanks anyway. I said that was great and then asked him what he loved most about the people he was already working with. He told me, and I asked what he wished they did better. After he told me, I said I'd love to meet with him and share how we do this if he was interested. I told him if he thought we'd be a better fit and serve him better that would be great, and if not that would be okay too. And I got the appointment!" Those kinds of things are priceless. I get that all the time now.

It doesn't take a lot to become a coach and you'll become a better and better coach the longer you do it. I'm definitely a better coach today than I was a decade ago. It's important for you to know that the coaching process starts as soon as someone hires you; they will immediately start getting better results. I've talked about this with other coaches. One of my friends who is a sales coach told me about his client, who once he hired him started growing like crazy, and he had only one session.

Sometimes it's not the coaching itself that makes a difference, but the commitment a client makes to himself or herself. Starting coaching with you means that they are committed to get this result and they're willing to put their money where their mouth is. That in and of itself starts the coaching process and starts making a difference in people's lives. And you *can* make a difference in people's lives. All it takes is a decision to do it, and maybe some of you have already made that decision in your heart. If you've made that decision, then take the next step, whatever that may be for you.

Remember, people hire you based on what they are going through, NOT based on who you are. Show up, be professional, and be there for your clients—they need you!

CHAPTER 13

What Are the Real Truths about Having a Coaching Business?

I'm about to share with you the hidden truths, the nitty gritty about the coaching business – the things you might not read anywhere else.

Upsides

There are upsides and downsides to having your own coaching business and I'm going to share them both with you. Some of the upsides are:

- you get to be your own boss

- you have unlimited earning potential

- you have total freedom

- you have a flexible schedule

- you can be as creative as you want

You get to be your own boss. Have you ever had a boss who frustrated you, annoyed you, was incompetent, or drove you crazy? No more do you have to deal with other people being your boss. I didn't like it at all. I had one boss I loved and several I didn't like. The one I really enjoyed had a huge impact on me in building my confidence and self- reliance. Other bosses I've had drove me crazy. You don't have to deal with bosses. That's the real upside.

Add to that **unlimited earning potential**. With most jobs, you might be able to make six figures, but I think the average median salary across the US is probably somewhere around $42,000 a year, maybe less. Even if you can make $100,000 a year in your coaching business, that's a lot higher than the average wage earner.

I was looking at the median CEO's salary in San Diego, which is just under $300,000 a year, which is quite a lot of money for most people. But coaches can make that much. I interviewed someone who was a participant in one of my group coaching programs about three years ago, and he's grown his coaching business to over $300,000 a year. I know coaches who are earning more than $1 million a year, myself included. There is really no limit to how much money you can make as a coach.

When you have a coaching business, part of the money you make is going to be from working with people one-on-one, but you can make a lot of money through group coaching as well. This is one way to make coaching more affordable for those who can't afford one-on-one coaching. With group coaching instead of working one-on-one, you have two to twelve people.

If you can work with people in group settings, instead of people paying you $1000 or more a month, now they're going to be paying you $200 (or whatever amount you choose) a month, but they'll be in a group program and you have six people paying $200 a month. Now you're making $1,200 a month and you might have three one-hour coaching calls. For three hours you're making $1,200 and that's $400 an hour. There are lots of ways you can grow your income.

A lot of people teach how to have a coaching practice with only one-on-one coaching, but my philosophy is you want to have a variety of income sources. I started out doing mostly one-on-one coaching, then eventually did group coaching, and it was a long time before I had any products and programs for sale, but the sky is the limit. That is a huge upside to having your own business—unlimited earning potential.

I used to be in sales and I used to get maybe 10% commission—10% of everything I sold, and that was actually pretty good. Then I realized when I would sell my own coaching programs, I got to keep all the money! When it comes to a coaching business, there is almost no overhead. You have a phone line, you might have a website, you have office supplies, and maybe some advertising costs, but compared to other businesses, there is really almost no overhead. Most coaches coach from their home, but you can really coach from anywhere in the world. I could coach from Hawaii, and I've done that many times in the past where I've been on vacation and still did my coaching sessions. Now, however, I'm at a point where when I'm on vacation I'm not coaching anybody.

Also the freedom and flexibility of your schedule is a great upside to your own business. I've gotten to the point where I usually work Monday through Thursday and usually in the mornings only; I don't work on Fridays—I take three-day weekends. I remember when I was in school thinking, wow, weekends should be three days long and the regular week should only be four days. And now, I've created it for myself. You have that kind of freedom to do that when you have your own business—a totally flexible schedule.

You also get to be very creative. I love what I do. I love my business. I love creating new products and programs to serve people, like this book. This is fun for me. This is creative. This is great. I get to do what I love and be creative—all the time. It's fun writing articles, teaching teleclasses, coaching, and creating new programs for my clients—they're all creative outlets that are so fun. I love it. You can create products to sell online like audio or video products, eBooks, courses and programs, or teleclasses. You can be very creative doing all sorts of things when you have your own coaching business.

Downsides

Of course, every business has its downsides. Some in the coaching business are:

- having to learn sales and marketing
- experiencing uneven income

- ramp-up time can be three months to three years

- constant failure, learning, and growing

If you want to be successful in coaching, you must learn sales and marketing. As I see it, these are two halves of the puzzle. **You need to learn how to coach, and then you need to learn how to get clients**. If you want to know why some coaches fall out of the pipeline—they become coaches and then give up—it's because a lot of coaching schools don't tell them they've got to learn sales and marketing.

I really think the schools ought to let their students know that graduating usually isn't enough. Although, since there are some coaching jobs, perhaps the schools don't feel a responsibility to inform their potential students. Therefore, they don't go into the business side of coaching or how you're going to get clients. And they don't talk about the downsides of having a coaching business.

In fact, a friend told me that at one of the biggest coaching schools they told her, "You'll probably charge around $300 a month for each client, and you'll be able to work with about 30 clients a month." If you do the math, 30 clients times $300 is $9,000, and multiplied by 12 months you're making six figures. Then they said, "There are 10 billion people on the planet so how hard could it be to get 30 of them to become your clients?" But most coach training companies aren't going to tell you the reality of it: you need to learn sales and marketing to get those 30 clients!

Sales training doesn't need to be expensive, and it doesn't need to take years. It's taken me over a decade to learn all I know about sales and marketing, specifically how to get coaching clients. A lot of that was trial and error. I had a lot of business experience with other businesses and what it takes to get clients, but each business is different. You need to learn the specifics of the coaching business. Thus, the downside is, not only do you need to learn coach training, but you need to learn sales and marketing.

I'm saying it's a downside, but the truth is that the people who make the most money in the world are the ones who know sales and marketing.

It's really worthwhile to learn the skills. I teach these skills in a way that as you sell and market to people, you also serve them. And it becomes an enjoyable process, one that you feel good about it.

Lots of times people have a hard time with sales and marketing, because they feel like they're supposed to tell how great they are and boast about their service or product, or they have to be pushy or do things that are outside their comfort zone, or out of integrity. And that's totally not true. You can learn to sell from integrity because you believe in the value of your service. Yes, you do need to learn sales and marketing and I include it as a downside only because it's not generally taught. However, I think it's really a huge upside because those are skills that will serve you well for the rest of your life, and with the right attitude, it can be fun.

Another downside is uneven income, and that's only a downside when it's low, because once it gets to a higher point and its uneven income, then it's okay. Gee, I only made $10,000 this month, while last month I made $20,000, but I know I'll be making $18,000 the next month. That's not too bad! But the first few years of my coaching business, I didn't have a lot of money to be able to invest, and there weren't even a lot of programs back then on how to grow your coaching business that were any good.

I had to do it the hard way, it took me a long time, and that uneven income was very challenging, very difficult for me. There were months when I was behind on my mortgage because of uneven income, while in a couple of months I'd be making good money and things got better, and then I'd have a couple of bad months. That's definitely one of the downsides.

Another downside is the ramp-up time to grow your coaching business. At first, it can be something you do part-time on the side—it doesn't have to be your full-time business. For me, not only did I not have a part-time income, but I had a bunch of debts. I went into it and really had to scrape and claw and work hard to get clients. But ramp-up time can be anywhere between three months to three years depending on how much training time you need and how much business development you need to get a solid income developed from your coaching business. Now I say three months to three years, but I have a client who went from zero to six figures in three months. I know that's pretty rare, so I'd say most coaches are probably going to take between six and 18 months to be earning a great income. Some certainly take longer and some go faster.

The last downside is constant failure. As you learn anything, even if you have the best teachers—you could be learning karate, you could be learning basketball, you could be learning anything. You're going to be failing a lot. You're going to be making mistakes. You'll be failing over and over again.

I cannot tell you how many things I've started and failed at, how many programs I've attempted to launch that fell flat on their face. I have failed over and over again and actually, I think Michael Jordan has said that he's missed more than 9000 shots in his career, lost almost 300 games. 26 times he was trusted to take the game winning shot and missed. He's failed over and over again, and that is why he succeeds!

I'm listing this one as a downside, constant failure. There is no doubt about it, no skipping it, you're going to make a lot of mistakes, and it's just part of the learning process. However, the upside of this is that it's the ultimate personal growth arena and you will grow through each mistake as you learn from them. Being in your own business, having your own business will grow you. You'll become a stronger person, a more confident person, a richer, deeper person by going through these trials and challenges and coming out on top.

I'm still going through the process, and I still make mistakes. Certainly I make less and less as I grow, and the mistakes I make are smaller and smaller, but I still make them all the time.

I used to have a job some people would have never quit, where I was getting paid to do almost nothing. My work took about an hour a day, and I was getting paid to sit in front of my computer for eight hours. I could surf the Internet, I could make phone calls, I could do anything I wanted, as long as I sat in front of the computer all day. And I was getting paid to do that. A lot of people would say, "Hey, I'll take that." But honestly, that was the unhappiest time in my life. In fact, that's when I decided to hire my coach. My life was miserable and coaching was my savior.

What are some of the other reasons coaches fail in this business besides ongoing mistakes or learning experiences? I would say one of the first things is that they were uneducated from the beginning about having their own business. They don't even think about the whole "getting clients" part of the business. When I started my first business, I didn't even see the whole picture; I just started working it and jumped right in.

That happens to a lot of coaches. They might get introduced to coaching from a friend or from a coach training school and no one really tells them that not only are they going to have to learn how to be a coach, but they're also going to need to learn how to market their business, get clients, and grow their business. I think after they get done with their coach training, they figure they'll get serious about it once they get certified. Once they get certified, they figure they'll get serious about it once they get their website and their business cards; then once they get those, they'll try to find something else to hide behind. They might dabble in it a little bit more, and have some struggles and think maybe they're not good enough and need more coach training.

A lot of what coaches are taught to do in their coaching businesses either just doesn't work, it doesn't work too well, or they're taught to do the wrong things. Let me give you an example. We've talked about giving out free coaching sessions to give prospects a sample. You want to do it in a way that really shows people what coaching is about and the value of coaching. If you just give out a free sample of coaching, then you don't get clients hiring you very often, you may start wondering, "This is what I've been told to do by the coaching schools, and it's not working. Maybe I'm not a good enough coach and need more coach training." It's not exclusive to the coaching world. That's one of the biggest reasons for failure, not having the expectation up front that getting the coach training is only the first half; the other half is getting the business training.

Another reason coaches fail is they get caught up in their own stuff and maybe never get through it. There will be tests where you're going to have to sell for the first time, and market yourself, and ask for the money, and maybe do public speaking, or write articles, and get feedback. Or, maybe you start getting a few clients and get a few new leads and then start second- guessing yourself.

Coaching is probably one of the biggest "head-game" businesses you could ever start, but I also think it's one of the most rewarding and fun. There's also a lot of freedom—for me, I wouldn't have it any other way. I've had other businesses, and this is by far the best thing I've ever done.

That's why I'm such a big fan of coaching and why I'm teaching you about coaching, because I think it's one of the greatest things on the planet. It's one of the greatest forces for change on the planet. I simply love it. It's changed my life ten times over for the better.

I grew up on food stamps, with public aid, and was in a bad financial situation growing up. To be where I am today, with a million dollar coaching business, working four days a week, doing what I love for a living, making a difference in people's lives—I wouldn't be here if it wasn't for all the coaches who coached me along the way. Definitely my first coach and several of the coaches I've had since then have made a big difference in my life. I'm coaching's biggest fan and I'm a huge believer. And I believe in you!

Remember, people need our help. Let's get people coached!

CHAPTER 14
Coaching Books

These aren't necessarily books on coaching, but these books have taught me a lot that I have applied to my coaching practice.

The Alchemist, Paulo Coelho

Awaken the Giant Within, Anthony Robbins

The Celestine Prophecy, James Redfield

The Four Agreements, Don Miguel Ruiz

Laws of Spirit, Dan Millman

Loving What Is, Byron Katie

The Mastery of Love, Don Miguel Ruiz *The Pilgrimage*, Paulo Coelho *Unconditional Bliss*, Raphael Cushnir

Way of the Peaceful Warrior, Dan Millman

I've also written another book on coaching that you might want to check out:

Get Clients Today: How to Create a Surge of New, High Paying Clients Today and Every Day

CHAPTER 15
Resources

Coach Training:

Here's a list of coach training offerings. It's not a complete list. There are 3 coaching schools that I know of that are not listed here. The people who own this list get a commission from some of the schools. It's great to be able to check out the different programs out there, but remember that the list may be biased and features some schools more prominently. That said, it's the only list I know that has so many schools in one place. **http://tinyurl.com/y4kk9a**

I created my own coach training program that people are raving about called "Rapid Coaching Academy". You can check it out here --> **www.RapidCoachingAcademy.com**

Enrolling Clients:

This is something I think every coach should have. The program in-cludes detailed step-by step instructions teaching you a 7 step system on how to enroll clients from that initial free session. **Free Sessions That Sell** shows you a way to create lots of value in and impact for the potential client, and also a way to clearly communicate what coaching is so that people want to hire you, right on the spot.
http://www.FreeSessionsThatSell.com

Growing Your Coaching Business:

This is my main program for coaches who want to grow their coaching business quickly. The **Client Attraction And Money Making Mas-**

tery program includes tons of 'done for you' materials and templates to make it as easy as possible for you to grow a thriving coaching business. **http://www.ClientAttractionAndMoneyMakingMastery.com**

Coaching Associations:

ICF www.CoachFederation.org

IAC www.CertifiedCoach.org

IMPACT http://www.IMPACTforCoaches.org

Your Next Steps:

I highly recommend the **Rapid Coaching Academy** program, especially for coaches who want to get started right away and don't want to spend tons of money and tons of time. This program is really going to help you to deliver coaching and feel confident and competent with what you're doing. If you already feel confident and competent in giving people the results they desire through coaching, I would say go for Free Sessions That Sell or Client Attraction And Money Making Mastery. For coach training, I invite you to join me in the Rapid Coaching Academy. **http://www.RapidCoachingAcademy.com**

Want to know if you'd make a great coach? Go here to take the 60-second quiz: **http://www.CanICoach.com**

ABOUT THE AUTHOR

Christian Mickelsen is a leading authority on personal development and personal coaching. He's the author of *How to Quickly Get Started As a Personal Coach: Make Great Money Changing People's Lives*, *Get Clients Today: How To Get A Surge Of New, High Paying Coaching Clients Today And Every Day*, and the upcoming book *The Solution To All Of Life's Problems*.

He's been seen in Forbes, Yahoo Finance, MSN, and the Boston Globe.

He's the founder of IMPACT - the world's leading association for personal coaches

As a personal coach for over 13 years and a trainer of coaches, he's helped countless thousands around the world experience the life changing power of coaching. He's on a mission to get the whole world coached.

He lives in San Diego, California with his wife and two daughters.

Find him here:

http://www.CoachesWithClients.com

http://www.ImpactForCoaches.org

http://www.ChristianMickelsen.com

http://www.facebook.com/christian.mickelsen

http://coacheswithclients.com/twitter

http://coacheswithclients.com/facebook

http://coacheswithclients.com/linkedin

Or contact him at Coaches With Clients:

Christian@CoachesWithClients.com

619-320-8185

Made in the USA
Las Vegas, NV
19 December 2023